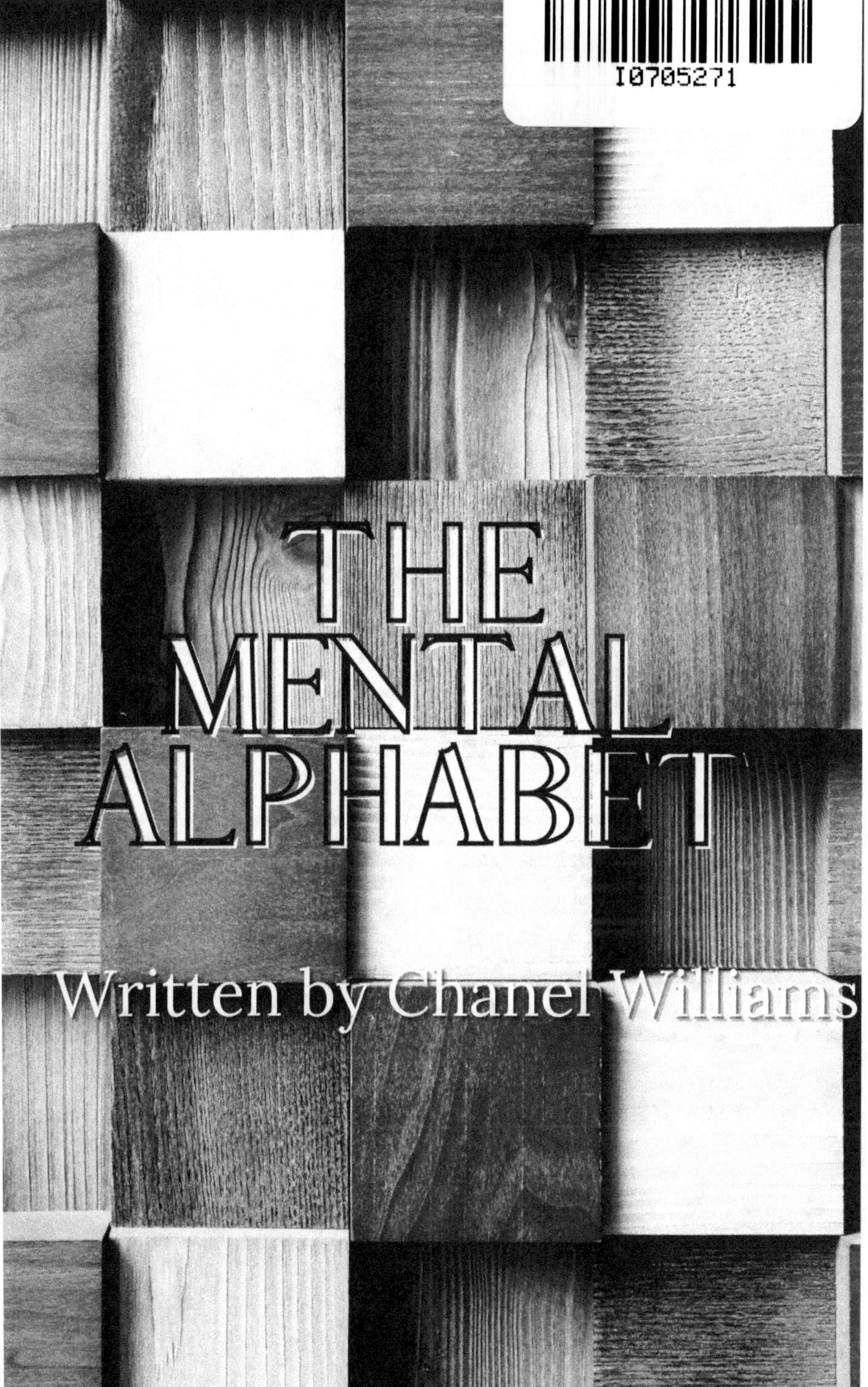

THE MENTAL ALPHABET

Written by Chanel Williams

THE MENTAL ALPHABET

Written By Chanel Williams

A
is for Attitude.
What's your attitude today?

B
is for Brave.
When is it time to be brave?

C

is for Calm.

What helps you stay calm?

IS FOR DEFEAT.

Will <u>IT</u> defeat you, or will you defeat IT?

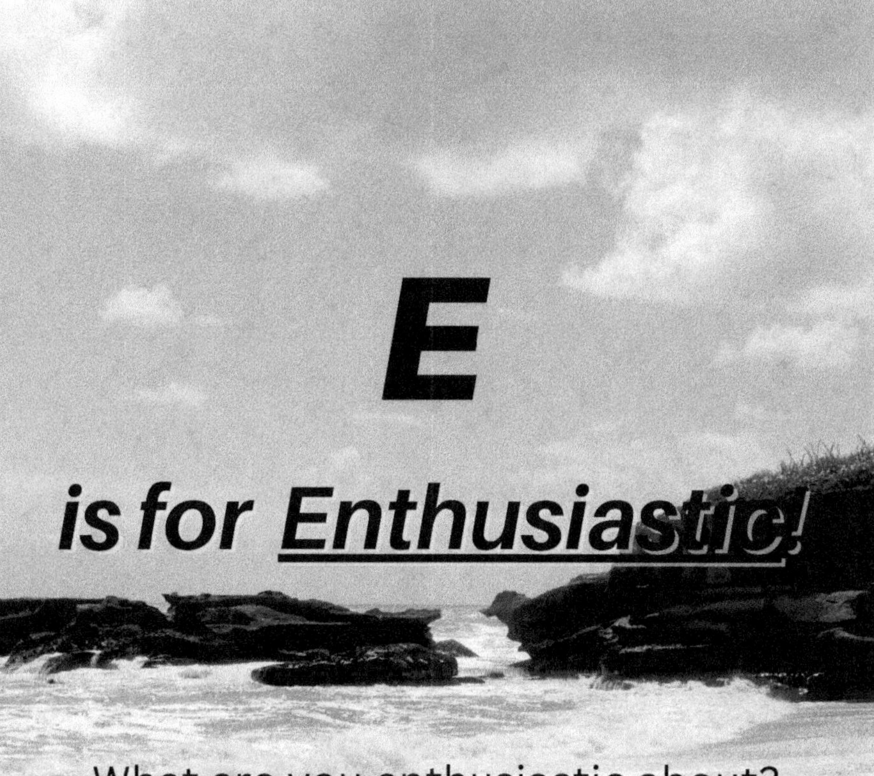

E

is for _Enthusiastic!_

What are you enthusiastic about?

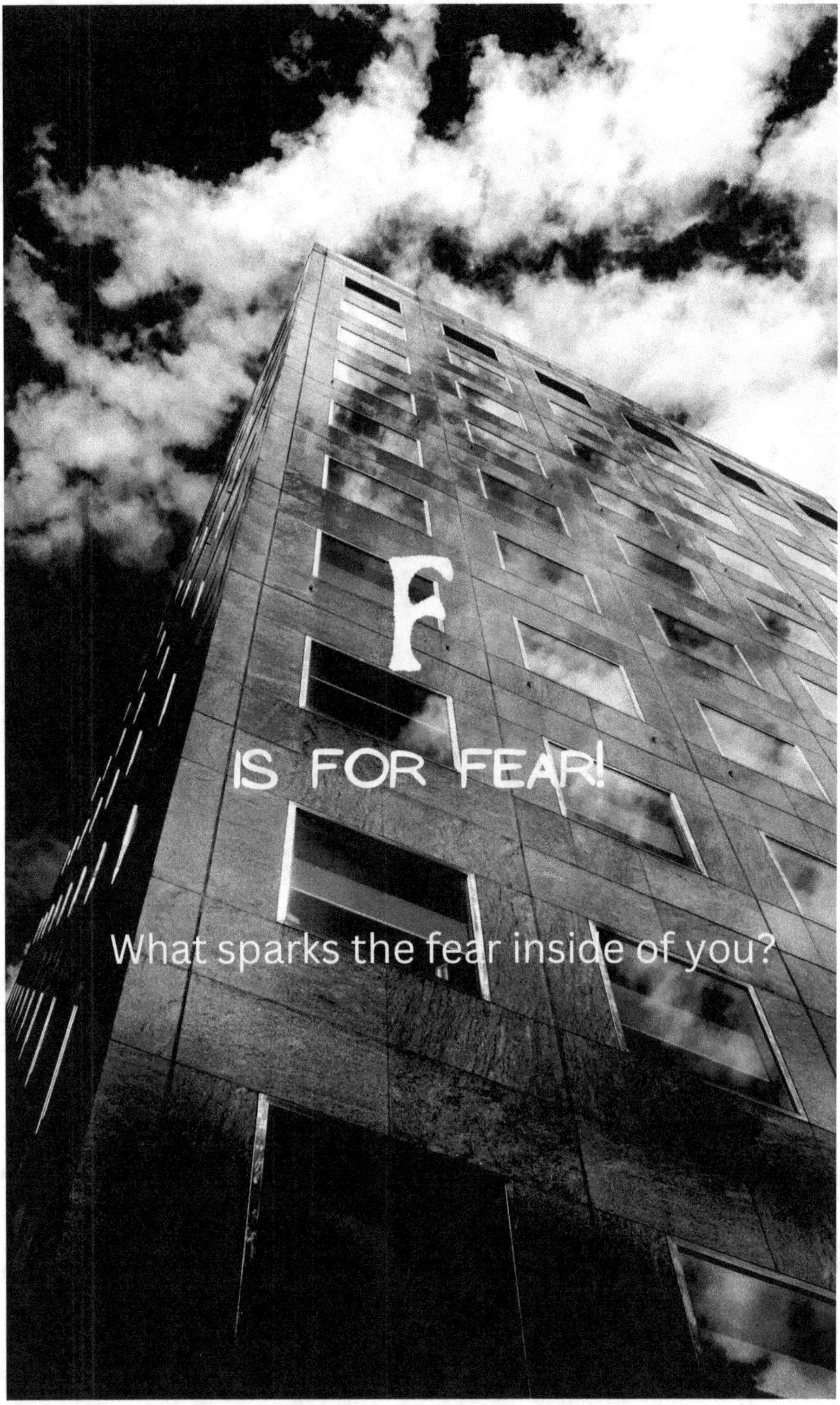

F
IS FOR FEAR!
What sparks the fear inside of you?

G

IS FOR GLUM.

What makes you feel glum?

H

IS FOR HEART.

What do you do with all your heart?

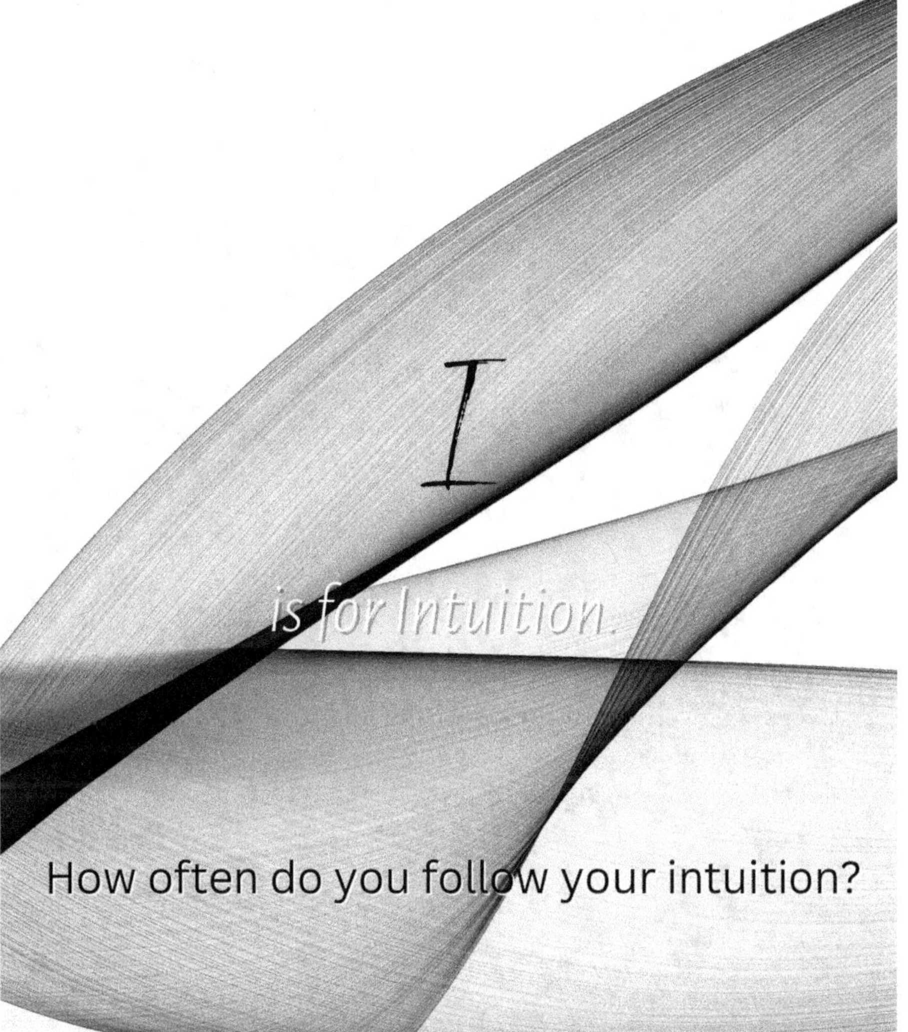

How often do you follow your intuition?

J

IS FOR JOY.

What brings you joy?

K

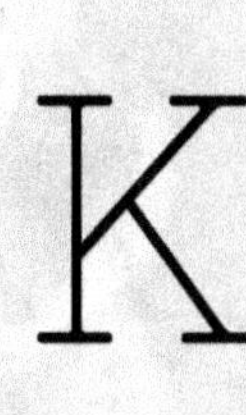

is for Kind.

Are you a kind person?

L
is for Loyalty
How do you measure loyalty?

M

is for Mindful.

What should you be more mindful of?

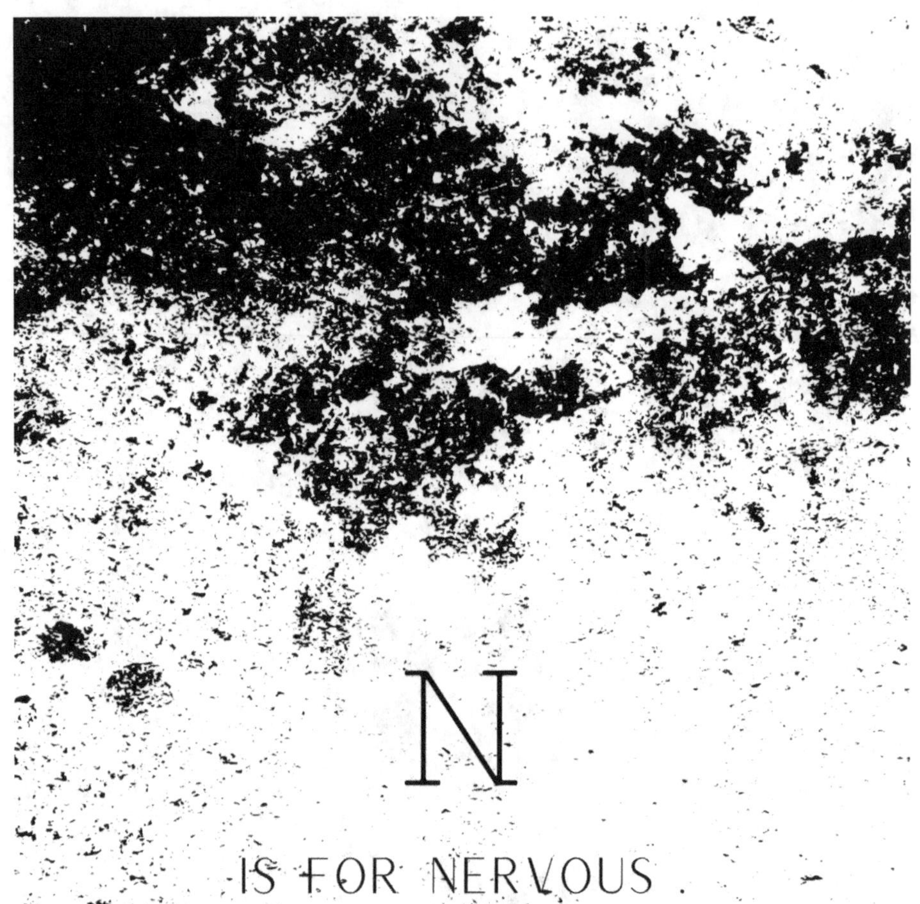

N

IS FOR NERVOUS

What is the one thing that always makes you nervous?

IS FOR OPTIMISM

Are you optimistic?

P

is for Proud.

What makes you feel proud about you?

is for Quiet

When should you be quiet?

R

is for Rage

What triggers you to feel in raged?

S
is for Soul

Are you in-tune with your soul?

T
is for Trust
Who do you trust?

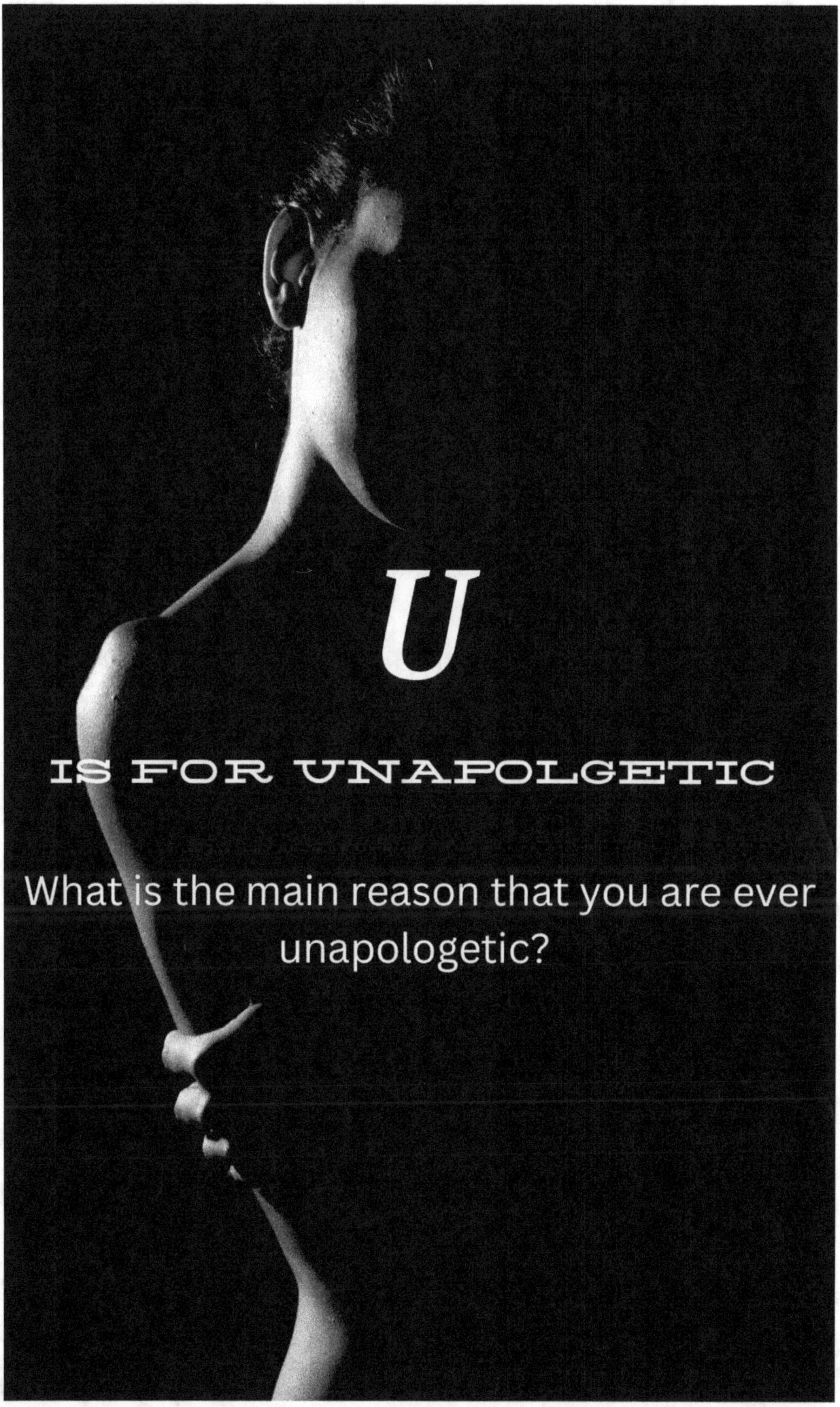

U
IS FOR UNAPOLGETIC
What is the main reason that you are ever unapologetic?

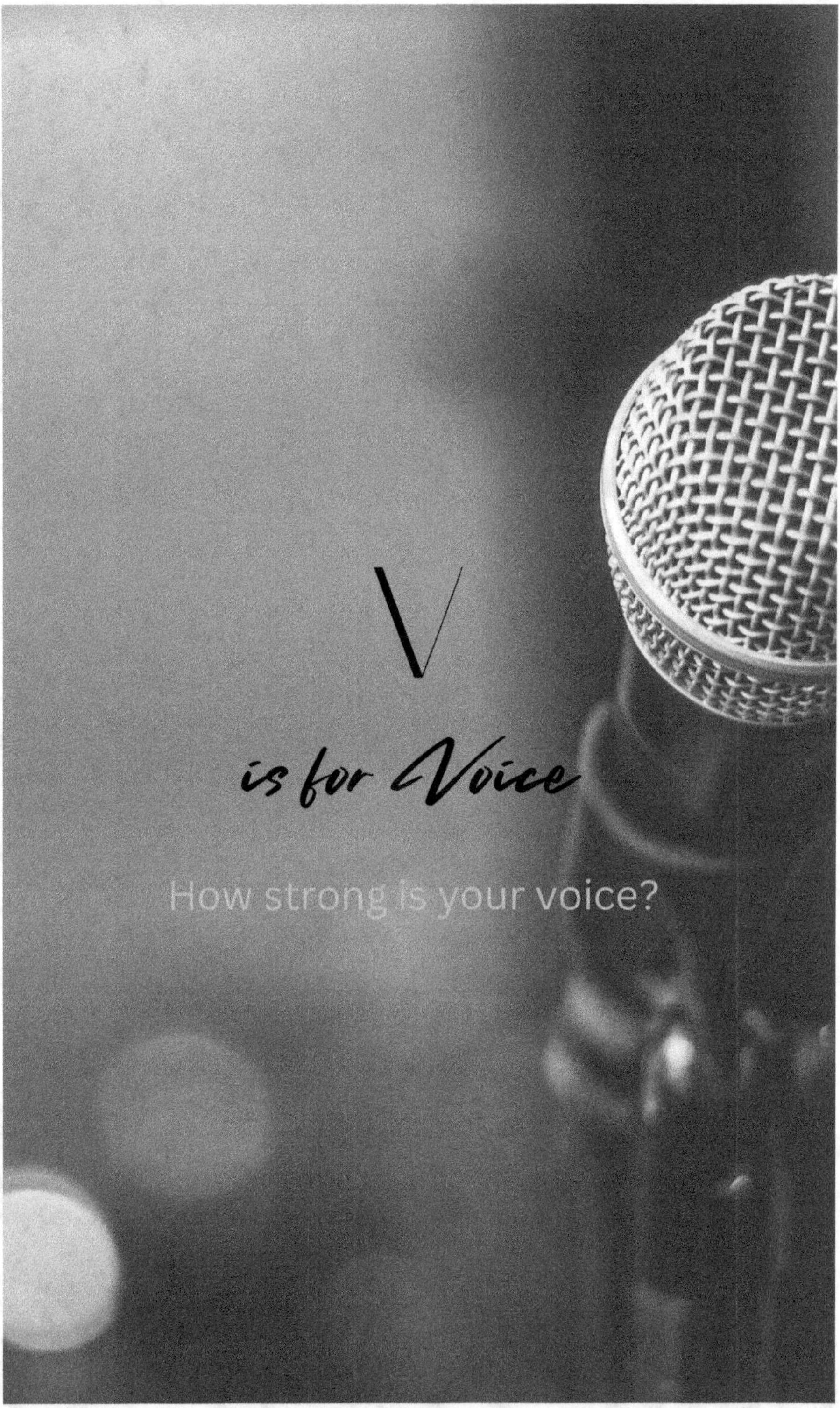

V

is for Voice

How strong is your voice?

IS FOR WISDOM

Who do you turn to for wisdom?

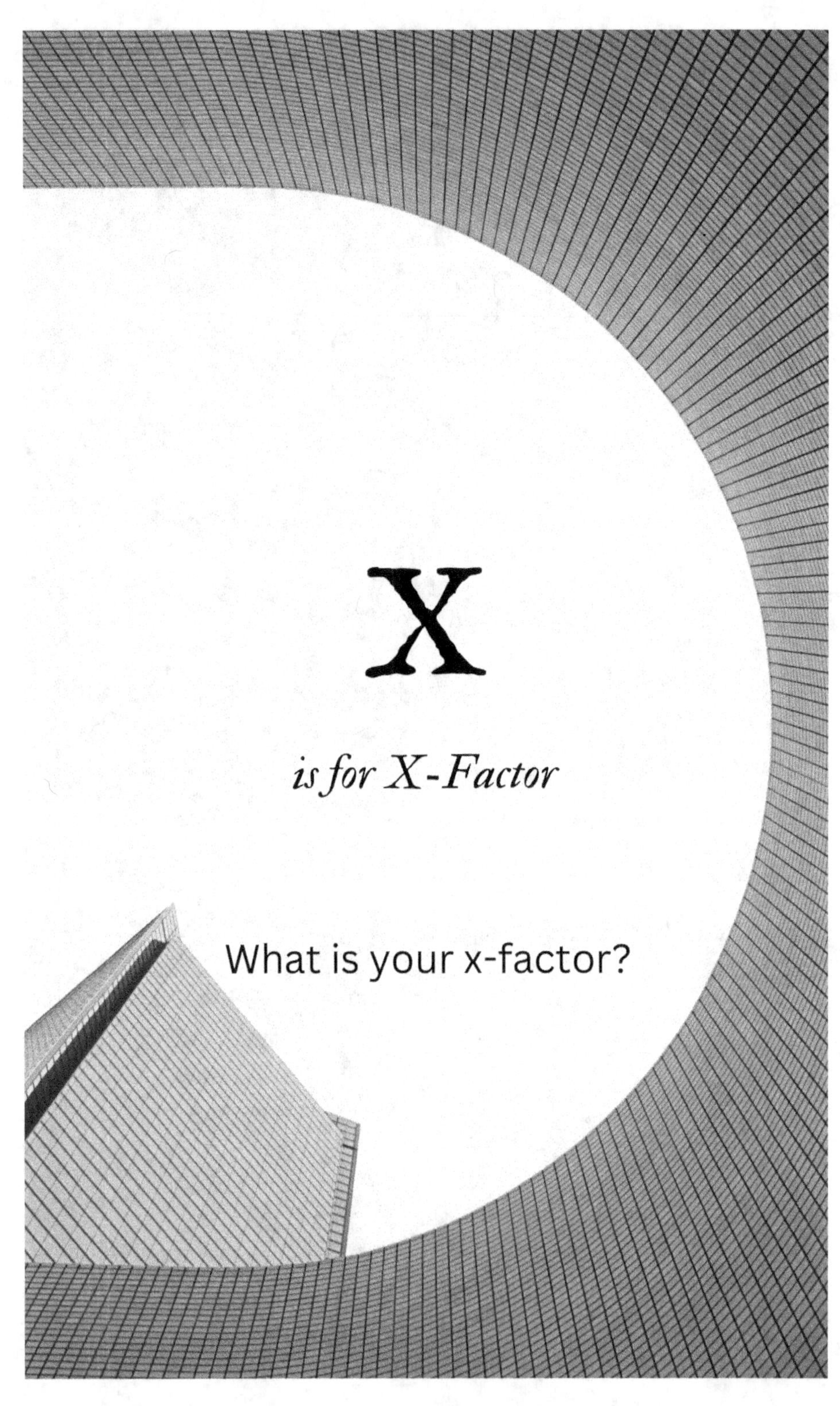

X

is for X-Factor

What is your x-factor?

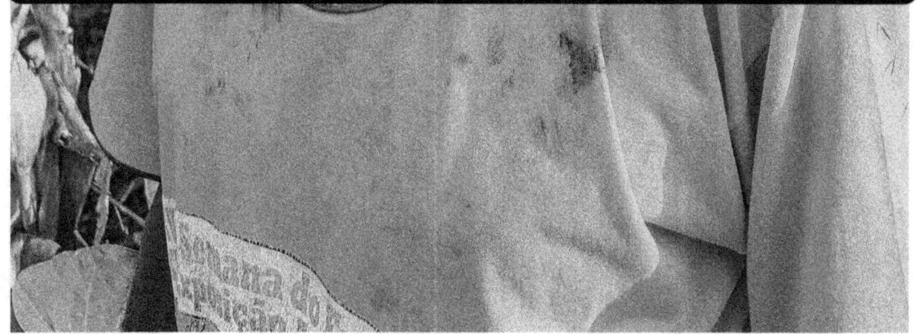

is for Youthful

What do you practice daily to keep your youthfulness?

Z

IS FOR ZEAL

What triggers the zeal to come out of you?

MESSAGE FROM THE AUTHOR:

YOU ARE VALUED

You Matter. You Are Everything! How you feel matters! There's always someone out there that LOVES YOU!

The End

with Love.

* 9 7 9 8 3 6 9 7 6 6 9 1 0 *